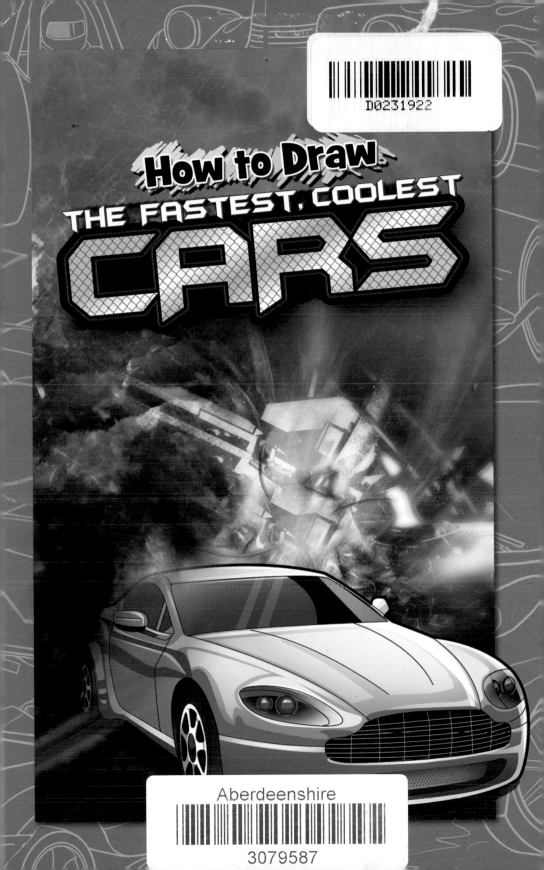

How to Draw
THE FASTEST, COOLEST
CARS

www.raintreepublishers.co.uk
Visit our website to find out
more information about
Raintree books.

To order:
☎ Phone 0845 6044371
🖷 Fax +44 (0) 1865 312263
🖳 Email myorders@raintreepublishers.co.uk

Customers from outside the UK please telephone +44 1865 312262

Raintree is an imprint of Capstone Global Library Limited, a company incorporated in
England and Wales having its registered office at 7 Pilgrim Street, London EC4V 6LB
Registered company number: 6695882

Text © Capstone Press 2011
First published by Capstone Press in 2011
First published in paperback in the United Kingdom by Capstone Global Library in 2012
The moral rights of the proprietor have been asserted.

ISBN 978 1 406 24295 9 (paperback)
16 15 14 13 12
10 9 8 7 6 5 4 3 2 1

British Library Cataloguing in Publication Data

Singh, Asavari.
How to draw the fastest, coolest cars.
743.8'9629222-dc23
A full catalogue record for this book is available from the British Library.

Author: Asavari Singh
Editor: Laura Knowles
Art Director: Joita Das
Designer: Deepika Verma, Isha Khanna, Navneet Kaur
Colouring Artists: Aadil Ahmed Siddiqui, Abhijeet Sharma, Danish Zaidi, Priyanka Singh,
Madhavi Poddar, Vinay Kumar Sharma
Line Artists: Deepak Kumar, Ishan Varma, Martin James, Nishant Mudgal, Prithwiraj
Samat, Surendra Kumar Tripathi
Originated by Capstone Global Library
Printed and bound in China by Leo Paper Products Ltd

CONTENTS

CHAPTER 1
GETTING STARTED 〉〉〉〉〉〉〉〉〉〉〉〉〉〉〉〉〉〉 4

CHAPTER 2
SPARE PARTS 〉〉〉〉〉〉〉〉〉〉〉〉〉〉〉〉〉〉〉〉 10

CHAPTER 3
SPORTS CARS 〉〉〉〉〉〉〉〉〉〉〉〉〉〉〉〉〉〉〉〉 16

CHAPTER 4
LUXURY CARS 〉〉〉〉〉〉〉〉〉〉〉〉〉〉〉〉〉〉〉〉 20

CHAPTER 5
EVERYDAY CARS 〉〉〉〉〉〉〉〉〉〉〉〉〉〉〉〉〉〉 24

CHAPTER 6
RACE CARS 〉〉〉〉〉〉〉〉〉〉〉〉〉〉〉〉〉〉〉〉〉〉 30

CHAPTER 7
INNOVATIVE CARS 〉〉〉〉〉〉〉〉〉〉〉〉〉〉〉〉 38

CHAPTER 8
CAR FASHION 〉〉〉〉〉〉〉〉〉〉〉〉〉〉〉〉〉〉〉〉 44

FIND OUT MORE 〉〉〉〉〉〉〉〉〉〉〉〉〉〉〉〉〉〉〉〉 48

CHAPTER 1
GETTING
STARTED

From ferocious Ferraris to classy Cadillacs to speedy racing cars – there are so many great cars on the road. And you can learn to draw them all! Just practice these drawing techniques and step-by-step projects to learn the skills you need to make realistic sketches of your favourite cars.

Types of cars

There are many different categories of cars, each with their own unique features:

Sports cars: They have large wheels and **spoilers**, a sleek shape, and usually have just two doors.

Luxury cars: Plush interiors and stylish grilles, fenders, headlights, and bonnets set them apart.

Tuners: These are everyday cars that make a statement with their unusual design or custom features.

Race cars: There are many different types but almost all are slim, streamlined, and ride close to the ground.

Alternative cars: These high-tech vehicles may fly, float, or push other boundaries!

spoiler: wing-like device attached to the back of a car. Spoilers help a car's rear tyres grip the road.

dragster

tuner

5

Proportions

Think inside the box! Start your masterpiece with a basic box shape. Drawing within this framework will help you get **proportions** right.

Side view

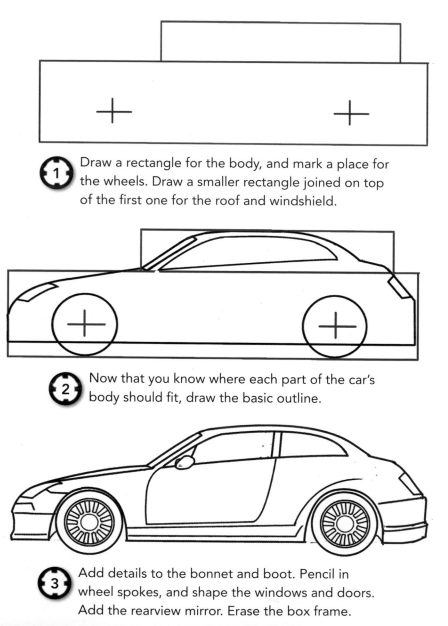

1 Draw a rectangle for the body, and mark a place for the wheels. Draw a smaller rectangle joined on top of the first one for the roof and windshield.

2 Now that you know where each part of the car's body should fit, draw the basic outline.

3 Add details to the bonnet and boot. Pencil in wheel spokes, and shape the windows and doors. Add the rearview mirror. Erase the box frame.

proportion: size of one part in relation to another

Front view

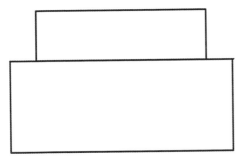

1 Draw shorter, thicker rectangles this time. This is because you can only see the front of the car, not its length.

2 Shape the bonnet, roof, and headlights. You can't see wheels clearly from this angle, so simply draw two undefined shapes at the bottom.

3 Add the number plate, grille, and wing mirrors.

>>>>>>>>>>>>>>>>>>>>>>>>>>>>>>>>>

TIP
Trace photographs of cars to get a feel for the kinds of lines and **contours** you will need to make when you start your sketch.

>>>>>>>>>>>>>>>>>>>>>>>>>>>>>>>>>

Perspective

Draw cars from different perspectives (points of view) to give them a more realistic look.

One-point perspective

Parallel lines seem to join at a single point in the distance. This is called the vanishing point (VP). To make a 3-D box using this perspective, first draw the horizon line and mark the vanishing point in the middle. Draw lines extending on an angle from that point. Then make a box within those lines.

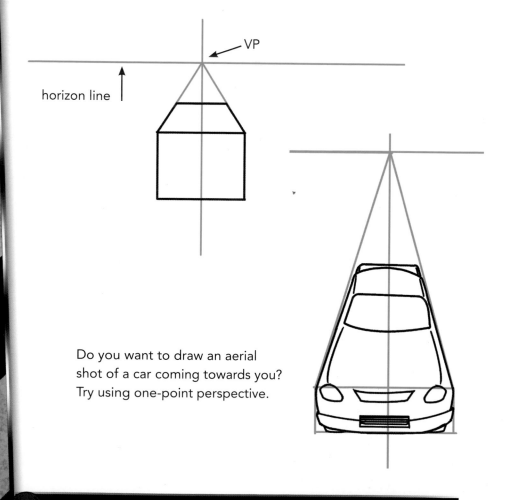

VP

horizon line

Do you want to draw an aerial shot of a car coming towards you? Try using one-point perspective.

parallel: two opposite lines that extend in the same direction and never meet

Two-point perspective

Use two-point perspective to show an object from an angle. Since two sides of the object are visible, there are two vanishing points. Draw lines extending on an angle from both of these points. Then make the box within those lines.

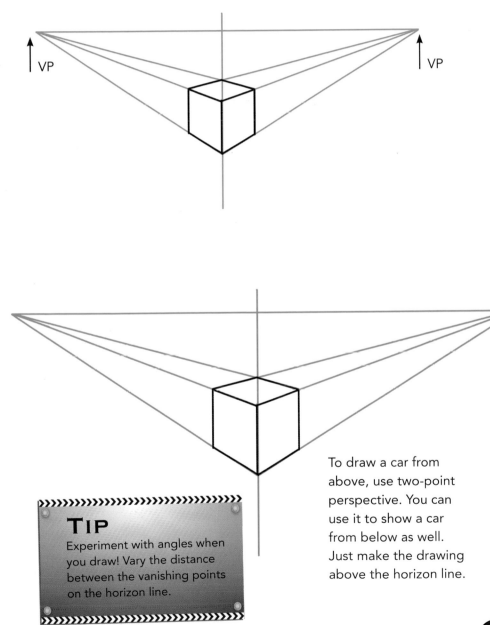

VP

VP

To draw a car from above, use two-point perspective. You can use it to show a car from below as well. Just make the drawing above the horizon line.

>>>>>>>>>>>>>>>>>>>>>>>>>>>>>>>>

TIP

Experiment with angles when you draw! Vary the distance between the vanishing points on the horizon line.

>>>>>>>>>>>>>>>>>>>>>>>>>>>>>>>>

CHAPTER 2

SPARE PARTS

Great details make an awesome picture. Car parts are just as important as the body, so pay attention to perspective and proportion when drawing them.

Wheels

Wheels are a big deal. If you don't get these right, your drawing could look awkward. A good wheel begins with a perfect circle or **ellipse**.

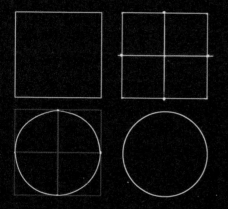

Circle

Begin with a square. Divide it in half, first vertically and then horizontally. Draw an arc in the top left quarter and replicate it in the other three quarters to get a perfect circle.

Ellipse

Use this shape when you want to draw a wheel at an angle. First, make a square in perspective and divide it into quarters. Draw an arc in the top left quarter and another below it to get a perfect ellipse.

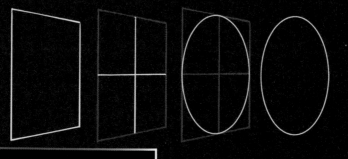

ellipse: circle drawn in perspective

1. To sketch your wheel, draw three **concentric** squares. Use these as guide boxes to draw concentric circles. For a 3-D view, begin with a cuboid, or box-like structure, and draw two overlapping ellipses.

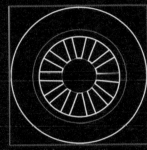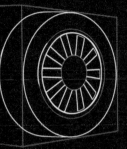

2. Define the tyres, the rims, and the hubcaps clearly. Draw spokes.

3. Add details to the wheels and erase any remaining guidelines. Add depth to the spokes to make your drawing more realistic.

concentric: describes objects, one inside the other, that share a centre

Glass act

Detailed surfaces on shiny glass parts can give your drawing a polished, professional look. Once you master the basics, try different shapes, sizes, and perspectives.

Headlights

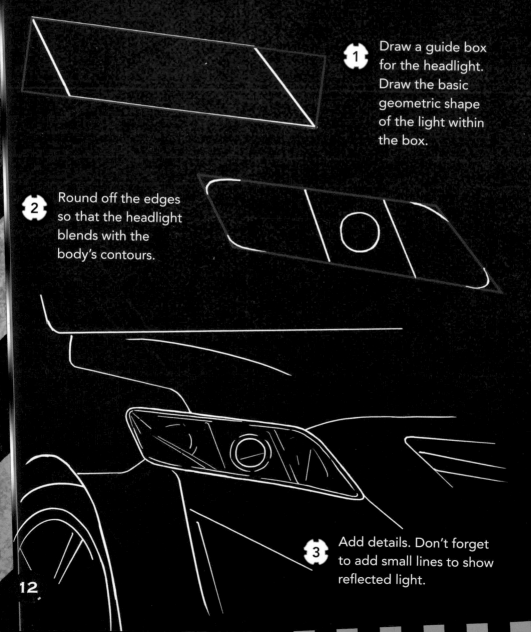

1 Draw a guide box for the headlight. Draw the basic geometric shape of the light within the box.

2 Round off the edges so that the headlight blends with the body's contours.

3 Add details. Don't forget to add small lines to show reflected light.

Windows

 Draw a guide box. Then draw a trapezoid, a shape that has one pair of parallel lines.

 Round off the shape so that the window matches the car's contours.

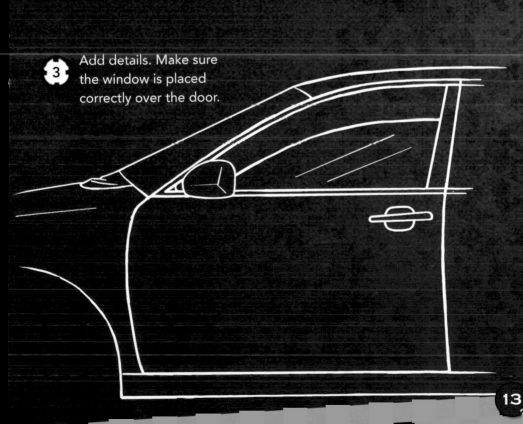 Add details. Make sure the window is placed correctly over the door.

Shading

Shading can instantly add depth to your drawing. It also helps show different textures and makes your art look more life-like.

Imagine a light source, such as the bulb below, before you begin shading. The part where the light hits the object directly seems brighter, while the other half is darker. The shadow of an object depends on the position of the light source.

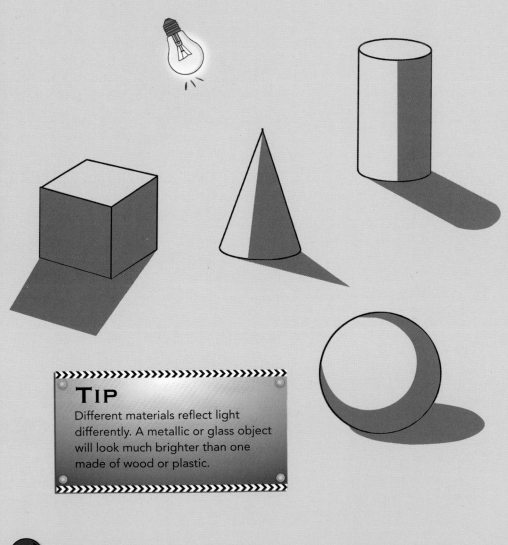

TIP

Different materials reflect light differently. A metallic or glass object will look much brighter than one made of wood or plastic.

The side facing the light source will reflect more light and appear brighter. The opposite side will be in shadow.

When the light falls from right above, the top half is **illuminated**. Pay attention to the contours, though. See how some parts of the car are casting a shadow.

CHAPTER 3

SPORTS CARS

> With their roaring engines and bold good looks, sports cars are shameless show-offs.

Modern sports car

This gleaming powerhouse is all about size and speed. Like most high-end sports cars, it can only fit two people.

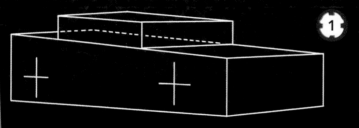

1 Draw two boxes for the body. The top one should be much narrower. Make the lower box narrower at the front than at the back.

2 Give the car a large hood, wheels, and a body that sits close to the ground.

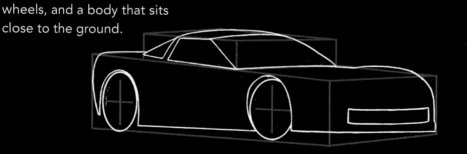

3 Draw headlights, a wing mirror, and the outline of the spoiler at the back.

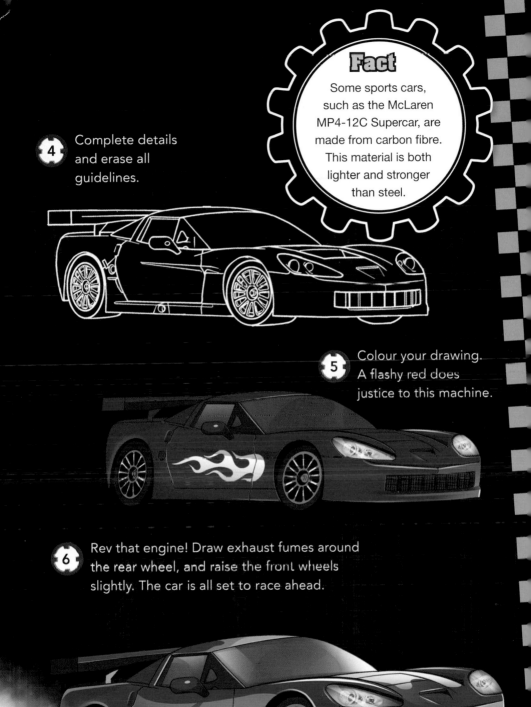

4 Complete details and erase all guidelines.

5 Colour your drawing. A flashy red does justice to this machine.

6 Rev that engine! Draw exhaust fumes around the rear wheel, and raise the front wheels slightly. The car is all set to race ahead.

Sports coupe

Also known as Berlinettas, these hard-topped luxury sports sedans have a sloping roof and showy curves. James Bond almost always drives cars like these!

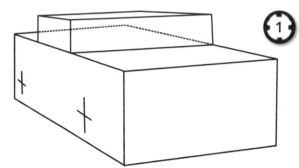

1 Draw two boxes and mark a place for the wheels. Make sure that the impressive front stands out.

2 Shape your sports car, and add large headlights, wheels, and a big grille.

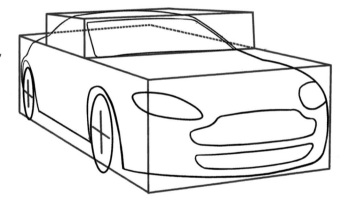

3 Complete the outline. Shape the wing mirrors. Erase the guidelines.

4 Add details to the wheels, and define the bonnet. Shade the chrome grille and add a custom mesh grille just below it.

5 Shade your drawing to bring out its sleek, shiny surfaces. Remember: the bottom portion is darker because it reflects the ground rather than the sky.

6 The colour of the glass will vary depending on the light. Use tints of white where light reflects off the metal and glass.

CHAPTER 4

LUXURY CARS

These stylish cars are status symbols. Packed with extra features and classy accessories, they cost a lot of money too!

Limousine

Limos are generally sedans with an extended chassis (frame) and four to six doors.

1 A side view of the limo will show off the car's length. Draw a cuboid for the body and another for the roof. Mark the wheels.

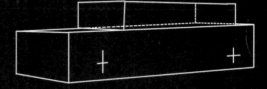

2 Shape the limousine. Imagine you are standing beside the car, but closer to the front.

Fact

The longest limo in the world stretches as long as 30 meters (100 feet) and has 26 wheels, a hot tub, and a helipad!

3 Add windows and details to the bonnet and wheels. Draw a wing mirror.

4 Add doors and details. Erase all unnecessary lines.

5 Black is a classic colour for limos. However, you can use shades of purple for parts that are exposed to light.

Convertible

Cool convertibles are perfect for those who enjoy the sun, wind, and making others jealous! A click of a button makes the roof rise from the boot or from behind the back seats.

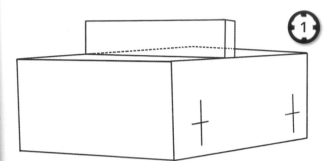

1 Make a large block for the body and a slim cuboid for the windshield. The wheels are large, so mark a place for them relatively high on the body.

2 Give the car a large, showy body. Draw the outline of the wheels, the headlights, and the grille. Add the outline of the steering wheel and seats.

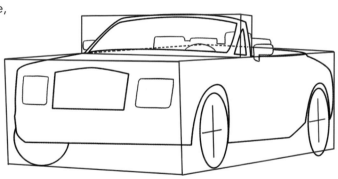

3 Detail the bonnet, wheels, and headlights. Add the door and define the seats more clearly.

4 Define the final outlines and details with a dark pencil or pen and erase any remaining guidelines.

5 Colour your drawing. Use white and grey tints to bring out the shine of the body and metal surfaces.

Fact

Some convertibles have windblockers that help keep the noise of the wind down. These also blunt the impact of rushing air.

CHAPTER 5

EVERYDAY CARS

> Even if you drive them every day, these cars are far from ordinary.

Microcars

These tiny cars zip around narrow streets with ease. They usually can fit only one person.

1 Start off this compact car with a single box. Mark out the wheels.

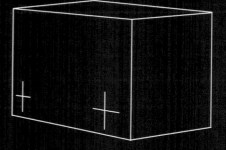

2 Shape the car within the box. The windshield and windows are relatively high on the body.

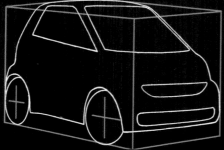

3 This is one curvy car, so round off the straight lines. Add headlights, wing mirrors, and details to the body.

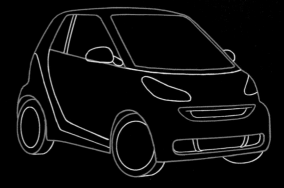

4 It's time to add all the trimmings, including wipers, wheel spokes, and details to the headlights and bonnet.

5 Choose a bright colour for this cute little car. Add graphics to the body to spice up the look.

Tuner

Spiffy spoilers, wacky wheels, and turbocharged engines are just some of the things people use to "tune up" ordinary cars.

1 Draw a two-box design for this sedan using two-point perspective.

 2 Sketch out the contours of the car. Add wheels and headlights.

3 Make a spoiler and add a wing mirror. Add details to the bonnet.

4 Complete the spoiler. It needs to stand out! Add details to the body and wheels.

5 Add finishing touches to the tuner. Erase any remaining guidelines.

6 Choose an attention-grabbing colour for this car. Bright pink can't be ignored! Add cool graphics to complete the look.

Get your tuner on the track. Make a blurred background to give the illusion of speed. The hot pink of this car helps show off the bodywork and glossy paint. Pay attention to shading. Use a lighter shade for the illuminated parts.

race cars

Crowds cheering, rubber burning, streaks of pure metal muscle zooming by – there are many reasons to love a day at the racetrack. No matter the type, each race car is built for supreme speed.

Indy car

This specialized speed machine roars around the Indianapolis Motor Speedway, USA at the speed of a cyclone. That's up to 322 kilometres (200 miles) per hour!

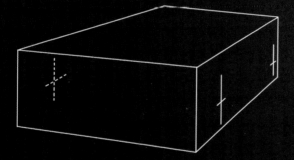

1 A single-box design is best for this **streamlined** car. Mark a place for the wheels.

2 Draw the contours of the car. It lies close to the ground to allow tyres to grip the road better. The long "nose" adds speed.

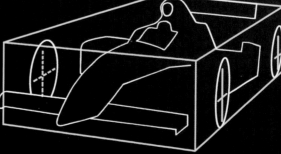

streamlined: designed to move smoothly through air

3 Define the wheels and rearview mirrors. Then erase the box.

Fact

Indy cars are formula racers. This means they must be built according to strict rules and be used only for racing.

4 Finish the shape of the car. The body is made of metal panels and has a large spoiler.

5 Complete the chassis (metal frame) of the body. This is what connects the wheels to the rest of the car.

Colour the car. Use a bright shade along with plenty of grey for a metallic look.

65

TM

No Indy car is complete without a number and some graphics and markings. Look up pictures of real Indy cars for design inspiration!

Top-fuel dragster

Dragsters can travel 400 meters (¼ mile) in less than five seconds. They are so fast they need to open parachutes to stop!

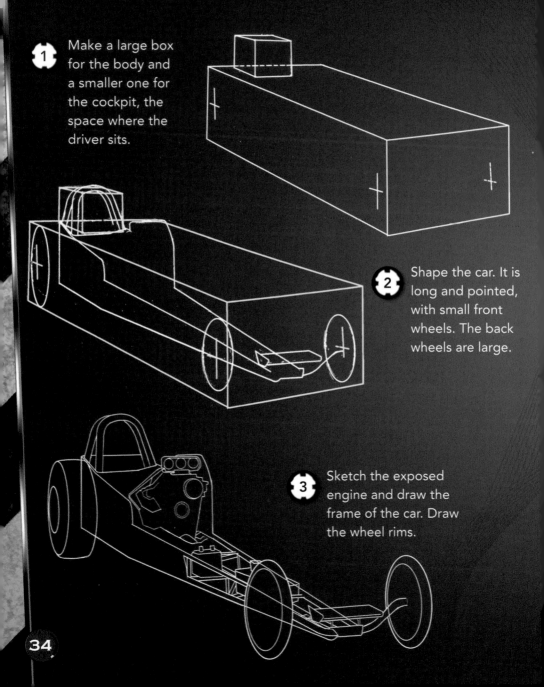

1 Make a large box for the body and a smaller one for the cockpit, the space where the driver sits.

2 Shape the car. It is long and pointed, with small front wheels. The back wheels are large.

3 Sketch the exposed engine and draw the frame of the car. Draw the wheel rims.

4 Add details to the wheels and engine. Draw a rough outline of the driver in the cockpit.

Fact

Top-fuel dragsters produce more than 30 times the horsepower of street cars.

5 Complete the wheels and give the driver a helmet. He needs it!

6 Complete the driver. Outline graphics on the car's body. Erase any remaining guidelines.

Give the car a number, and shade the graphics and helmet.

8 Colour your car and driver. Use greys and blacks for the engine and fuel tank. Choose bold colours for the body and graphics.

20

CHAPTER 7

INNOVATIVE CARS

Get off the road and cruise through water and air – without budging from your car!

Switch from land to water driving if you need to cross a body of water! The front wheels act as rudders.

1 Make two boxes for the body. Mark a place for the wheels – they are very low set for easy navigation on land and water.

2 Draw the shape of the car. Like a boat, it is broader in front and tapers towards the back.

3 Outline details such as the waterproof seats, steering wheel, headlights, and mirrors.

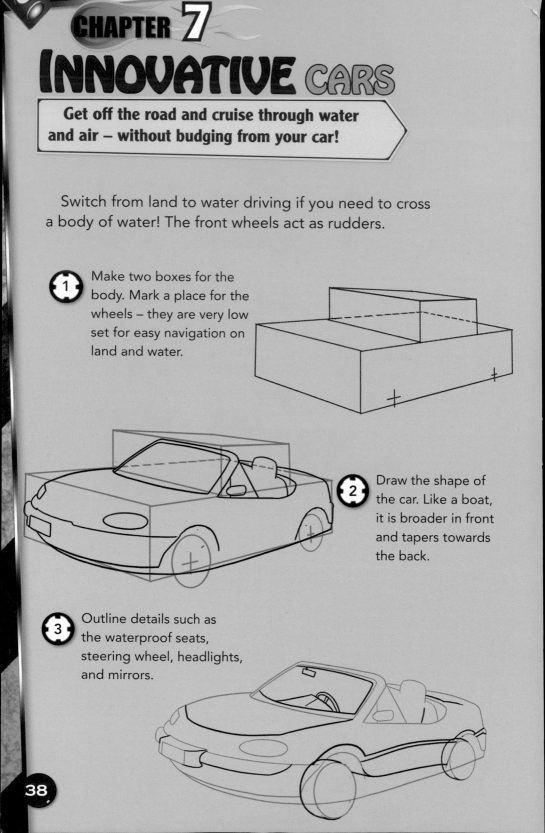

4 Complete the drawing and erase any remaining guidelines. You could add a driver, too!

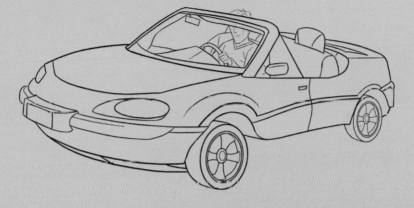

5 Colour the car. Show it cruising through water. Don't forget to add splashes of water around the rear wheels.

Personal air vehicle

It may soon be possible to rise above traffic jams and bumpy roads in your own flying car. NASA and some private companies are already developing designs for these vehicles.

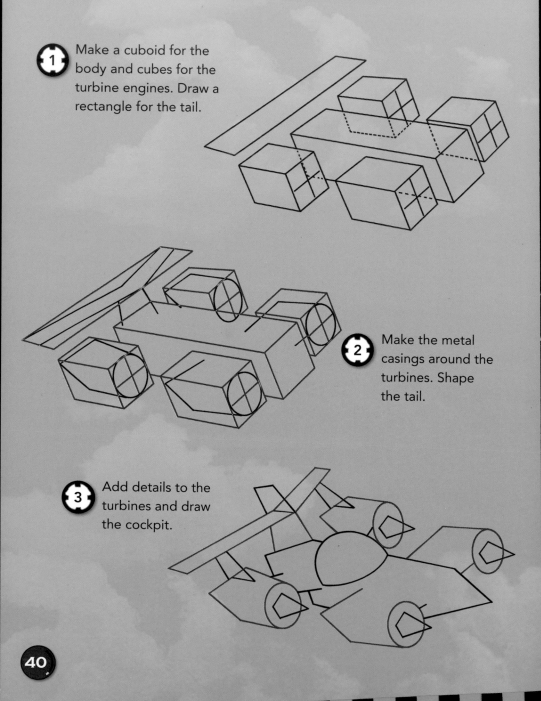

1 Make a cuboid for the body and cubes for the turbine engines. Draw a rectangle for the tail.

2 Make the metal casings around the turbines. Shape the tail.

3 Add details to the turbines and draw the cockpit.

4 Start rounding off the hard edges of the flying car to give it a more realistic look.

5 Add more details, including headlights, a nose, and a window. Spend some time on the turbines – they're the coolest feature!

6 Make the final outline with a dark pen. Add streaks at the back to indicate fast movement.

Colour the vehicle. Add a blue background and clouds to show it flying.

Use white to add details and shine
to the vehicle. Draw fine lines in
the turbines to make them look
as if they are moving.

CHAPTER 8

CAR FASHION

So what if you don't have your own car yet? Get creative with your car drawings. Customize them with sassy spoilers, bold graphics, and unique wheels.

Spoilers and wings

These features help cars stay stable on the road, but they also boost style.

1 This rear-mounted spoiler adds subtle style and is proportionate to the rest of the body. Spoilers can be attached to the front of a car, too.

2 A latticed stand for your spoiler is an easy-to-achieve design statement.

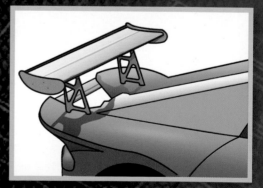

3 Wings are placed higher than a spoiler and create downforce. These massive add-ons can be more about fun than function, though!

Graphics

A bit of paint can give your car an instant makeover.

 Choose a place for your graphics, but don't overdo the artwork. Feathery wings sweeping across the doors add a creative flourish.

 These graphics add movement to the wheels even when the car is still.

3 Flame-inspired designs add a slightly dangerous look.

Wild wheels

Fancy hubcaps, custom rims, and designer tyres can add instant, eye-popping attitude to any car. Experiment with sizes, patterns, and finishes.

 A classic five-pointed hubcap would look great with a 1960s or 1970s model car.

 Get fast and furious with this spinning ring.

Add some star value to a
luxury car with this design.

This flower-power hubcap adds an
interesting twist to an ordinary sedan.

To find out more about cars, or to learn how to draw other exciting machines, why not look at some of these books.

The Car (Tales of Invention), Chris Oxlade (Raintree, 2011)

Car Science, Richard Hammond (Dorling Kindersley, 2011)

How to Draw Amazing Motorcycles, Aaron Sautter (Edge Books, 2007)

How to Draw Indestructible Tanks, Aaron Sautter (Edge Books, 2008)

How to Draw Mecha Robots, Mark Bergin (Book House, 2007)

How to Draw Monster Trucks, Aaron Sautter (Edge Books, 2007)

How to Draw Planes, Mark Bergin (Book House, 2006)

How to Draw Unreal Spaceships, Aaron Sautter (Edge Books, 2008)